THE WICKEN BIRD

Geoffrey Heptonstall

Some of these poems first appeared in *As It Ought to Be, Highland Park Poetry, Inclement, Littoral, Living Poets, The London Grip, Mediterranean Poetry, Meniscus, Other Poetry, Pangolin Review, La Piccioletta Barca, The Poet, Poetica Review, Poetry Monthly, Poetry Salzburg Review, The Recusant, Runcible Spoon, Taj Mahal Review, 10x10* and *The Write Place at the Write Time.*

Waiting was written for display at the Bolton Writing Festival 2011, and published in the festival anthology *Shop Window Poetry*

Day by Day They Unfold Their Secrets won the Avan-Ballan Prize in 2013

Tombland was the inaugural poem for Norwich UNESCO City of Literature in 2014

Musee Imaginaire appeared in the *Coffee House Anthology* 2016

Amelia Alone was read by Katiya Llardo as a podcast for *Loud Voices, Silent Streets* 2021

Several poems appeared in the anthology *Fixed Earth*, edited in Zimbabwe by Tendai Rinos Mwanake 2022

The Promise appeared in the anthology *Poetry for Ukraine* 2022

'Poetry may burn, but words will escape.' Lawrence Ferlinghetti

Contents

1. WORDS 7

TOLD BY FORTUNE 8

SPEAKING 9

CONSIDER THE WORDS 10

OUT OF MIND 11

WHAT OTHER THOUGHTS ARE FLOATING? 13

WRITING 14

FICTION 15

A FEATHER FELL DOWN FROM HEAVEN 16

WE SHALL BE CLEAR 18

ISLANDERS 19

FRIDAY 20

SCHILLER 21

HUXLEY, DYING IN CALIFORNIA 22

2. LIGHT AND DARK 23

WALKING THROUGH WALLS 24

MERE SHADOWS 25

STATE OF PLAGUE 26

TOMBLAND 27

TOWARDS THE DAWN 28

AMELIA ALONE 29

THE HOUSE IN THE FOREST 30

THE GARDEN: A RESTORATION 31

STOLEN FIRE 32

SONG 33

DARK WINE 34

SOLAR ECLIPSE AND MIDSUMMER MOON 36

3. IN THE AIR 37

CURRACLOE 38

THE GHOST MOTH 39

ONE FOR SORROW, TWO FOR SORROW 40

WHENEVER 41

BUTTERFLIES 43

THE WICKEN BIRD 44

A BIRD UNKNOWN 45

THE SALT MARSH 46

4. TRANSFERENCES 47

OF COURSE 48

LA MEMOIRE DU MONDE 49

AVIGNON 50

DAY BY DAY THEY UNFOLD THEIR SECRETS 51

LE PIN DORÉ 52

LES BALLONS 53

A MOROCCAN SPRING 54

EURYDICE 55

VERITAS 56

CHINA IN TRANSITION: A JOURNEY 57

NIGHT SONG OF THE PAVILION 57

FALLEN PETALS 58

A TIME OF WAR 59

5. A HOUSE WITHOUT WALLS 61

PICASSO'S LEMON 62

MUSEE IMAGINAIRE 63

AN IRISH ARTIST IN MEXICO 64

LANDSCAPE WITH THE FALL OF ICARUS 65

DANCER 66

6. TIME PASSING 67

THERE IS NO TIME 68

A GLANCE IN THE LOOKING GLASS 69

WAITING 70

THE PROMISE 71

CARTIER-BRESSON IN CAMERA 72

CAMBRIDGE 73

SOUNDS UNSEEN 74

THE AWAKENING OF STONE STATUES 75

A FAMILY HISTORY 76

WHAT MEANING MEANS 77

WHEN WILL THEY RETURN? 79

THE TIME OF MY LIFE 81

A GUIDE FOR TRAVELLERS 82

MORE THAN POSSIBLE 83

PENNILESS PORCH 84

OF ALL WORDS 85

1. WORDS

TOLD BY FORTUNE

There is a truth told by fortune
that what dies in the Fall
may return in the Spring.

Another country, so close at hand.
We name this promise as paradise
because there never can be an end.
It is the sense of a beginning
when there is no time to be
other than the elemental everything.
There is a time we cannot imagine
to still the hurry of things.
A wise word will surprise the world.

SPEAKING

Before we could speak there was noise
making no sense, but a stumbling
of tongues from toothless mouths.
All was known beyond a feeling
that we would come to see
the essence of things in view.

We might reach out to touch
the other land across the sound,
only to be caught in the current
under the monstrous roar
of words wildly searching
for an understanding voice.

We seek to speak what we hear within,
an echo of the word first spoken
making a universe of sense
of which at last we can speak
and be heard as easily
as the moment of time passing.

CONSIDER THE WORDS

In the moment of life itself
pale skin, once withered, quickens
when a moon sets on love-stained sheets.
Consider the words that have risen in mind.
See especially how sounds well-chosen
are floating on the morning's reflection,
voicing the energy released by chance.

Or was it choice at play this time?
This warrior's armour we need no more:
Words may decide their own meaning
from the tongues of fired minds
forbidding all temptation to silence
at the sign of the wonder of song.
The words naturally spring into being.

OUT OF MIND

Soon we discover the circle
could be a way to believe of course
if the answer is a transference.
I find eternity in my time.

Know it must be true
the unspoken beginning
is always changing.
Of all that can be known
only a portion is given
to say whatever pleases.
An explanation is waiting elsewhere.

The room is silent on the matter
that cannot be named for certain
in the realm of understanding
before the beginning was found.
The moment becomes
a reality revealed.
The truth is that truth was taken
by an opening eye
in the half-light of history,
being there through many lifetimes.

They will not hear your plea.
Who goes down and when
the elect will decide in the citadel
where life has distanced
the image from the flesh itself.

The choice we find where
there are no words
but whispers of the truth,
a relentless moving to explore
how the meaning changes
the shape of the line
when decisions are made
out of mind.

WHAT OTHER THOUGHTS ARE FLOATING?

What other thoughts are floating
in every possible world
when so many cities shimmer
in the water beneath our walk?

Another moon is rising:
It may be an omen.
The air is a void of silence
waiting to be broken
by a gathering of doubts
in the lost, high moon.

We are going to the gardens,
wondering where this city is
when we walk between worlds
now the moon has vanished.
Every traveller has a city
that every citizen dreams.

WRITING

Only when…
On this I give you my word:
only when read is a life real.
We know the signs of change
as they appear on the page
in words that reveal
how we learn to walk
through the wild land of words
that writing brings into being.

Of the unexpected…
We are what we write
of the mysterious, elusive,
a life of shapes and symbols,
refined into meaning
more than the here-and-thereness
of unexpected entrances
or a likely departure
when whispers dissemble the truth.

Of a time…
Our talent seldom lies
in the spoken word,
but in the felling of trees
and the tilling of earth
in search of a time
when it may be written
before the seasonal fall.
Then we see what we are.

FICTION

Always there is a story to tell.
Narratives float through the universe.
One may land on fecund earth,
and there become the spirit in the stone,
discovered, decoded and disclosed.
What is found is fabulous.
Writing, like love, impels
ordinary things to be other.
Everything is more than itself,
shadowed by parapets,
sheltered from the seasons.
Confessions stir the soul.
There are tales worth the telling.
In the reading room
by sunlit windows
diligent dreamers
read their secret histories.
Words are for winter light
distanced by choice,
peopled by silence.
The writer is alone,
especially in a crowd.
There are voices not his own,
though they speak what he has seen
when the candle of fiction flickers.
The story is never the same.

A FEATHER FELL DOWN FROM HEAVEN

Of Johnson and Boswell

It was a clumsy lump of a hand.
The words spoken were but half-heard
in the stumbling confusion.
'I am pleased by your countenance.'
A sentiment not aloud, but by gesture.

The click-clack of carriage wheels,
and an urban echo of horses.
Uncertain feet felt the London stones.
This was not his native pavement,
different in an indefinite way.

In the street the cockatoo screech
was the chancer's way of speaking.
His preference was for a purer diction,
of constructs in the plain and sturdy style,
as with the Doctor's imperative tongue

The voice was no other for sure:
the pounding of words on an island shore.
Poets brought their rhymes to the coffee house.
All was amassed for the lexicon
of fabulous places hitherto unknown.

Boswell's eye was taken with a serving maid.
Silk-stockinged, she might have graced the stage.
Naked, she would sail in his dreams.

His pleasures in life were varied.
The streets were shadowed at all times.

When a feather fell down from Heaven
the sound of the city was stilled.
A cloud passed over the sun.
'Sir,' said the Doctor, 'there will be a storm.'
And soon it came. Then it was dark.

In the calm that followed they walked,
determined on their course for ever,
A fellowship of spirit surpassing
mere circumstance of self.
'Your hand, sir. I have a liking for you.'

WE SHALL BE CLEAR

Reading Defoe's Tour of Britain

We shall be clear:
the balance between here and there
is but one way out.
In the main conventions die
in the chaos of an itinerary,
and the stream again runs shallow.

This town has nothing remarkable in it
for a stranger coming,
except for a gentleman's garden.
It was, if we believe antiquity,
a house of pleasure in more ancient times.
Of the house itself I may judge
as many windows as days.
Its ruins are all that is to be seen
where the mountains insult the clouds.

Meanwhile let us proceed
to see what we are not.
Within that swing the lines move
the tendency of revolt,
a siege of the familiar,
because people are what they are.

ISLANDERS

Crusoe

He carves the presence of each day,
savouring the thought of time
so constant in the rise and fall
of sun and tide and expectation.

A purse of silver buys nothing.
Wealth is ingenuity
inspired by survival
sheltering from nature
the rumours of universal Flood.
They feed his lonely fear.
Who else lives in this void
is no concern to merchantmen
passing on the horizon line.

The waves, they break in memory
of England and a seaport's graces.
An echo is a sign of life,
reflecting his own humanity.
He frames an arc of intentions,
an exchange of natures, of islands.

Friday

My name is not Forgotten.
Call me as I am now called,
named by my master
whose mercy saved me.
Owing him my life, I am owned.
I fear the wilder man in him,
the rage against this sacred land.

The beauty of freedom is flight
feathered in the colours of angels.
At night the demons sing
the songs of the dead I hear
from the embers of their pyre,
all flesh devoured in sacrifice.

Spirits return to their bones
discarded among the sand and ash
by the shore of the world's end.
My master is from another world
where the faces are ghostly pale.
I think he may be one of the dead
and cannot die again.
I dream of living my life.

SCHILLER

Writing well into the night,
he is moved to speak against silence.
A spectral twin accompanies him.
Then there is the opening door,
but no-one there when he turns.

In a salon the other side of the city
an adventuress dares to gaze on a rival.
A general orders his troops to find
the staircase he will climb alone.
The lamplighter sees more than he can say.

Sweet scent of apples and angels
enchant the writer's soul.
A poet does not seek peace:
in winter chill a spirit stirs,
in summer fields his passions rise.

HUXLEY, DYING IN CALIFORNIA

Images of an earlier England,
they floated in the dusk,
whispers in cloistered columns
so distant from the sun.
The trees he would never see again.
The contours of his thoughts were clear,
like starlight in the desert air.
The hour was close to infinity.

Something sacred rests in solitude.
A fire burns in the mind.
Searching, he seeks to reach the flame.
Cool winds over Pacific waves
drifting through the boulevards.
This is the day the world is made.

He ran barefoot, a child once more.
Reality shimmered in the city
where dreams are sold to the lonely.
A swan crossed the evening sky.
All his words were said at last.
Sunset saw the simple end of day.

2. LIGHT AND DARK

WALKING THROUGH WALLS

How easily when a window opens,
though a door may need unlocking.
Floating leaves find their way, escaping the rain
in the tidal wave of a sudden storm.
The wind begins gently, only to rise
as strangely as the cry of the wild
echoing on the walls inside the city.
The sound of the wind is stronger than stone,
air falling heavily in the heat,
an invocation of dark thunder,
loose shutters beating against the house wall.
Fear and anger pass through the rooms
to remind those within of what lies beyond.
All that seems secure is certain to fall.

MERE SHADOWS

Cast at first light against the sun,
its stretch of warning hands
move with the changes of time.
The tree is firmly determined,
but lichen quarrels with stone
on the crumbling of the wall.
Glimpse a human becoming
lizard-like in spiral ascent
to the far branches lost to sight
in the higher light of noon.
And silence the only sound.
No more the days of living
for another way down,
seeking reasons for being
more than mere shadows.

STATE OF PLAGUE

What if by a lightning strike
the tree is turned to stone,
soundlessly moving in moonlight?
We must feel an ending begin.
Another time we are released,
never to be heard again
through such restful sleep
if what happens is no more.
And wild, pale horses ride
when the day rises.
Things are not as they seem.
The world is not at peace.
The hand that grasps the nettle
from the blessing of certainty
takes the sting into its flesh
so close to the bone.
In time beyond the bounds
is the sound of birdsong
before the sun of the day.
This was not foreseen.
The darker the enchantment
the deeper down the long regret
Its light is not denied.
The circle has no ending.

TOMBLAND

Because there is no-one to speak
rising in the East and lightly
for the whispers of dust
we find the water flows
in the quarter of abandonment
there we follow in the spiral streets.

Across the city the wild child dances
into the Tombland taverns
where the lights are beckoning
from Adam to Eve and back again
by way of the well-worn track,
a secret within the heart of everyone.

And where the sun has gone
the saints consider their sins.
There you may find a change of mind
with the ever-approaching thought
that here was once another city,
on the way to somewhere or other.
The trail never seems to end.

TOWARDS THE DAWN

Towards the dawn elective,
cumuli of energy emerging,
day leaps from a lover's embrace
unembarrassed by nature.
What was distant approaches
in the universal custom
when the world is a sphere again,
enabling gravity to play the fool.
Rain falls as gently as mercy
from a mendicant's plea.
The light is lost in translation.
Truths are spoken in darkness
still within the shuttered room.
A promise opens fortune's eyes.

AMELIA ALONE

Amelia alone can dance the girl again
in her looking-glass room
where she may move through mornings
of her peculiar day
in this keepsake kingdom.

Behind an anonymous blind
a shuttered silence
and a lover's mouth opening.
Amelia dreams
her gracious unwisdom
never to know those things.

Be sure of certainties:
Amelia will not sing for you.
She has her songs
for those who sing with her.
Tree branches bow for her.

The swallows applaud.
'Encore' is the cry of cattle.
Nature is summoned,
indifference shamed
when Amelia sings of her love.

'I am Amelia,' she sings
in the deeps of the waking sleep
that has been all her life.
The life is hers no more.
Amelia is forever alone.

THE HOUSE IN THE FOREST

The leaves of previous summers
lie undisturbed in shadows
of this bell jar world.
The colours of the wood
are emerald and ochre
with shooting stars in mind
and a half moon even
in the morning sky.
Trees quiver in the chill
of an early frost sharpening the air
where desires are moving
through the open ground.
Shafts of sunlight soften
the earth which is Cezanne's
as seen by admirers:
An abandoned garden revealed,
and then the scattered stones
that once sheltered the dreams
of a hungry man.

THE GARDEN: A RESTORATION

A gathering of birds disperses
from this crumbling earth
in the dust of Eden,
seeking life on barren ground
with the first rain to fall.
Everything has something to ask
of the water on the stones.
Sky shades the rising flowers
so carefully planned and planted
with sharp spade and gentle fingers.

Unearthly eyes survey the land.
Tentacles of trees surface.
The hawthorn's beauty changes
the way of the garden world.
A crane fly floats on the water
as if to speak a quite truth
Songbirds rest on the silver bough
firmly holding all that we see.
The fig tree yields its secret fruit.
Nothing in nature is motionless.

STOLEN FIRE

She turns her head to the sound
when leaves fall out of season,
dry and brittle in the heat
of a relentless sun.
The air breathes out a stream of dust,
like sand in an hourglass .

Time is flowing away, leaving nothing
but endless, abandoned highways
beneath an infinity of clearness.
One day there will be cooling rain,
the tears of the world for its loss.
The gift of fire returns to the gods.

SONG

Spring storms fallen blossom,
a fearful leaving of home,
never to return.
Every leaf a butterfly crushed.
A long day's incessant rain
shipwrecks the white feather
floating on a shallow pool.
Jewelled ivy glitters in the sun.
The air is still and warm.

An overture of approval
from the mercy of the sky,
the clouds dispersing.
The sky that caught a falling star
was darker and lonely.
So clear in the mind
a wish to be fulfilled,
but not before a taste of frost
chills the fruit that grows in time.

DARK WINE

Their lies are written in laughter,
so silently heard.
In pain there is no choice.
Reality overwhelms
as if this moment were history
soon to be forgotten.
All the queen's horsemen are riding
On their way to war,
should one break out soon.
The appeal is to the banal
and the shame of it.
A childhood of lost innocence.

Where there was a wall
came a promise of liberty,
not mentioning the wounds.
They will haunt our expectations.
We are mariners drowning
when the familiar returns.
The scene has been rehearsed
inside the mind of the world
with 'spontaneous' applause
from everyone knowing their place.
That way no doubt lingers.
Further walls of fear rise.

Nobody asks what everyone knows.
Raucous calls from the gallery
set the tone of the night's enquiry.

The conclusion will be popular.
Of that we can be sure.
The wine flows freely, darkly.

SOLAR ECLIPSE AND MIDSUMMER MOON

A shadow passes the sun,
and the world slows down
as far as the eye can see,
a dark horizon that is not night
with no stars to guide the wanderer.
This is not travelling time.
The sounds of life are stilled
by the absence of light
on nature's understanding
of earth's relation to the sun.
It may seem the last morning
leading to the end of day.

On the evening of the day before
there was a moon that blushed,
a modesty within exposed,
her body swollen with promise,,
like a child in the womb,
waiting to inherit the earth.
The sun rose as if surprised,
a goddess aroused by the call
to arms in a time of danger.
Every dawn brings challenges
falling like rain in a clear sky.

3. IN THE AIR

CURRACLOE

A creature of the coastal waters
is the wader who watches each day
in shallow sea.
Who knows what she searches for,
always out on the cold shore?
Ripples of the tidal flow envelop her,
though her feet tell her to run.
One day, they say, she will drown.

THE GHOST MOTH

The ghost moth hovering
in the moonwatcher's mind.
Every creature a cosmonaut
in the stillness of night
through each phase passing
where a spirit in motion
is seeking signs of life beyond
the elusive bonds of time.
From one world to another,
lost again in nostalgia,
the flight is a long history.
The darkening sky at dusk reveals
a distant star rising,
moving closer to celestial light.
slowly, and at first alone.
The moth now sees its mission
in the shadows on the glass,
in the lamp that burns within.

ONE FOR SORROW, TWO FOR SORROW

The bird that sings a stolen song
leaves echoes of another sound
from a tongue bereft of voice.
'*Pica, pica*,' the magpie cries,
naming its nature in air.
Joytaker, heartbreaker,
what it sees it steals
in glistening desire,
feathered with wildness
to plunder the beauty of things.
The joker in a pack of lies,
it lives on sorrow alone.

WHENEVER

Of an architectured ending
I see angel fingers wakening
a future in exquisite designs,
I wait for your touch on my face.
I think of conversations
where I walk down again.
A flight of birds shall pass
in my imagined sky

There are so many streets ahead.
Always the same hour chimes
the moments of thought,
knowing I am still far away.

In a desolate mansion
I find myself stumbling on stones
as sharp as the knife that slices.
My eyes do the talking
in regular rhythms
reflecting the moon rising
somewhere that is not here.

Voices whisper in my sleep,
careless in what they say.
So often the song I sing
fades like yesterday's wishes
away from varieties of whatever.
To live for all the years
where I hear no more of now,

nor of any time but then
whenever there may be time.
There are no calendars in memory.

BUTTERFLIES

Their wings speak in many tongues.
A clouded yellow in the hedgerow
flutters from the ripening flower
Against the hope of landing.
They have endless time to fly
with restless minds wandering
always in faith across the world.
All that is light in skyward glances
gives a sense of direction
on unmapped highways.
We travel toward infinity
on reflection rising
beyond a lifelong expectation
that reason can never fulfil.
We find ourselves nowhere,
a promise of certain means
in the conquest of fear,
from time to time and again
named in the art of memory
seeking earth's inspiration.
The rain as sky's ocean flows.
There will be fruit to taste soon.

THE WICKEN BIRD

A glimpse of feathers in the reeds.
And the air carries the spring's return
where the rain tastes of the sun
when other birds are sought
from the world beyond.
An instinct conferring grace
over land and water
passing through nature's dreams
prepared for a life of flight.
The marshland melody foretells
a future watchful and winged,
an ancestral enchantment
woven in a thread of grass.
We search the sky for signs
only the clear eye can see
for the coming season
of beauty and strength in song.
In the bird world lovers are chosen
to bind desire in harmony.
All else is curious intrusion,
A cuckoo's egg, of course.

A BIRD UNKNOWN

A bird unknown flies from the moon.
The machines begin their working day.
From here the vantage is godlike,
remaking the worn, weathered city
with imprints of the unexpected
in their higher rising image
over the world's outstretched hand.
All is everything we can see
that is at times starlit.
There will be no rain
when we lose our hereafter.
Through the dawn the sleepers dream
an impression of sunrise
that lingers through the hours
to the close of one day
soon transformed to another.

THE SALT MARSH

The heron finds a haven on an islet
while clouds sweep over the salt marsh
to cover the moments of light
reflected in myriad pools
when the sun burns through sea winds.

The heat of the day has lost heart
There may be seen rising
a moon from out of the water.
So fabulous a detail
is true to us in feeling.

Impression pictures a cinnabar sky
with seabirds in silhouette
on the marsh and the long shore
that here defines the borders of land
across the arc of the bay

Where sky and land are one
the sea slowly approaches
following its tidal nature.
All we see is infinite horizon.
All we hear is hidden from view.

4. TRANSFERENCES

OF COURSE

That it must be true
there is the question
with firm advice to see why
a sudden transference appears
if that is the answer.

A future self beginning.
the unspoken something,
almost the essential *'Of course'*,
widely admired by changing minds
in various guises.

We can see the reason advanced.
A circle could be a way to believe
In time we discover
an approach so personal
we ask no more questions.

LA MEMOIRE DU MONDE

Maintenant le monde ouvert
parce qu'ici est la vérité
de faire le sens enfin.
Un conte est contre raison,
un roman sans les mots,
l'histoire impossible
d'être humain dans l'univers
qui garde le silence partout.

Unreal as it seems,
there is a truth in this
that opens for you
where there is a door.
Tempted to take a last glance,
all you see is darkness.

What is never spoken
is being human in the world,
the unlikely story,
a text without words,
a narrative of the mad.
And yet it makes sense
because here is the truth
that opens everything.

AVIGNON

L'amour, toujours une résonance,
suit bientôt le familier certain
bruit d'une fièvre matinale,
la musique d'une chanson inconnue,
un chant des enfants.

Considering the world
is all within the walls
well made of shadow and sun.
Light in the waking of life:
this is how the day begins
with cold candle wax tears
and wine lingering in the glass.
Love, always a resonance,
soon follows the familiar certain
sound of a morning fever,
the music of an unknown song.
There are children sounding
like the sea, in the trees
a winter away from the sun
when souls rest from seeking
a peace that speaks no more
in terms of pity, in time of war.
That is the blood that flows
dispelling doubt through the dust
pale as ancestral memory
of distant, other places –
a rumour across the delta
where land and ocean confide
the enchantment of return,
the redemption of the real.

DAY BY DAY THEY UNFOLD THEIR SECRETS

Day by day they unfold their secrets
in becoming delicacy.
Women with their parasols
swaying in the wind
which speaks through the open door.
You have arranged them
in the sunlit crystal vase
on the white-tiled table
where talkatively we eat
among the flowers I found
and the music you chose.
They bloom in the harmony
of instruments and voices.
Their colour is rich and
as pleasing as a generous smile
without fear of storms.
A tremor of war sounds as
the world out there is shaken.
Everything alive is whispering.
The women alone say no
more than their need allows.

LE PIN DORÉ

This first light snakes through the shutters
soon after the music,
a song she shall hear all day,
a perfect blue painted from the sea
beneath the sun.

Yesterday the Mistral raged
in sand and swaying pines,
and raised an army against her.
Frail world in the dark sky.
Today there is still life, serene.

LES BALLONS

Les ballons des enfants de la ville
se soulèvent comme les vœux des oiseaux
sur les toits du paradis.
Les chapeaux des grandes dames
tombent dans une tornade.
Maintenant je marche vers le parc
en attendant un autre saison,
une époque d'un printemps pour toujours
quand la lune est pleine
et le ciel est un million des étoiles.
Je compris les yeux de ton espoir.

Understanding hope in your eyes,
I see the million stars of the sky
when the moon is maternal,
a time of eternal spring.
Now I walk to the park,
waiting for another season
I watch the hats of great ladies
in the storm that falls.
Balloons float in children's minds,
like the wishes of birds nesting
on the roofs of heaven

A MOROCCAN SPRING

Sand drifts in the high wind
as thought falls from the tree
before the fruit can ripen.
At dusk the air is stilled.
A celestial sound settles
on those perfect harmonies.
Or so it seems to sleepers
woken by the call to remember
a single-stringed instrument
making intricate music
as if to move the crane birds
floating through the clouds.
A song may find its way down
on one note as long as night
fading into a cool, dry dawn.
This way the day begins well.

[Inspired by Ahmed Harrouz, artist and poet of Essaouira,
Morocco. His studio is in a tower of the ancient walls overlook-
ing the Atlantic. Ahmed's meditative poetry is collected in
L'Essence des Sens.]

EURYDICE

All is to a purpose clear
when slowly she rises
as if she were the sun
lighting the cold, clean air
that sees the death of pestilence
facing a fearful world.

Beauty to a candle flies
not knowing how danger lies,
to go down again suddenly
in a slip of the tongue.
Voices below echo the oracular
sharp as a serpent's sting.

Fine sounds escape the fires
when attentive ears take care
of an unearthly music.
From the lyre an arrow flies,
a shooting star that falls
as she fades into herself again.

VERITAS

Questions:
they ask for an answer
hovering over the oracle well
beneath the thorns entangled.

Reasons:
they remain mysterious
sounds from the spring of purpose
revealed by light on deep waters.

Truth:
she is found where least expected,
always obscured by an absence
of vanity in distorting glass.

The geese, they guard the citadel
from time to time, a history
written in the watchtower.
Only then do we find a way down

Veritas, the Roman goddess of truth, was sequestered in a well.

CHINA IN TRANSITION: A Journey

NIGHT SONG OF THE PAVILION

The river level rises with the moon
bringing the frosted air
as the third watch sounds
over the tidal flow
shaking the fishermen's lanterns,
starlight on the dark water.

A lute's melodious song
surrounds the ghostly pavilion.
A merchant's wife follows a lonely life
among the spirits of travellers..

My boat glides silently
in search of lost souls.
I sail into infinity,
like the poet of past times.
But the lute is quiet.
Fish and dragon sleep.

(From Tsu Fu 1751-1833)

FALLEN PETALS

The garden is still and silent
after the festival of flowers.
An aroma of wine lingers
on the petalled ground.
At the sunset hour the rowan fades.
At last light an easterly wind will rise
to cool the flesh among the rowan flowers.
The spring has a sadness,
like clouds that shake the blossom,
blowing away as new leaves form.

(From Chiang Ch'un-Lin 1818-1868)

A TIME OF WAR

To the hero his fame,
not fearing what will not endure.
For the hero the sword
that cuts not once but again
The time of glory passes,
not denying youth its victory
when the wise shall rule.
But when the serpent wins
all we see is war.

(From Huang Hsing 1874-1916)
Rooted in antiquity, Imperial China declined in the Nineteenth
Century as the West advanced. The poetry of China, though
maintaining traditional forms, began to reflect the move towards
change and revolution.
In these three poets we can trace the development from tradi-
tional themes to a sense of a new dawn. The last poet, Huang
Hsing, was active in the revolution of 1911, and a close associate
of its leader, Sun Yat Sen.
These versions are not translations but adaptations.

5. A HOUSE WITHOUT WALLS

PICASSO'S LEMON

The fruit he takes from the tree
with branches overhanging the track
leading upward to the mountains.
Later, by the stream,
he severs the lemon
in six equal slices,
one for every hour of his walk.

A lifetime passes in a day.
The prospect of the fertile plain
looks unexpectedly alien.
The artist is a long way from home.
His vision will be exiled
perpetually, making him one
forever discovering
loss and regain
in signs and shapes,
and the reviving scent of lemons.

Everything anatomised
is thereby forgiven.
He takes charcoal to paper,
and hears his minotaur.

MUSEE IMAGINAIRE

In other words there is love
regarding the way things may seem.
A door is opening onto infinity.
A woman is perpetually posed,
anticipating a change of light.

There has been a fading.
The colours have changed.
and so, too, her expression
since last we saw her.
But Bonnard left the door ajar forever.
It was all he could do.

Art is a house without walls.
All who pass may look inside
in daylight, or in darkness
when there is *splendor*
to guide the uncertain eye
to see that this how things are.

Elsewhere the walls have fallen
when imagination began
to pass surely through.
A moustached attendant
rises from his dutiful indifference
to build another wall with silence.

AN IRISH ARTIST IN MEXICO

All day is noon.
Every canvas burning
when he patterns the Day of Creation
displayed on a gallery wall.
I am led here by the art
of someone I knew.
He had a studio in the garden
beneath my shuttered window.

Harmony, I tied to find her,
to see the world made plain.
This art is at war with another world.

The heat of life moves him.
The eye of Phil Kelly
soon sets the scene in innocence:
and to feel no pain,
but to harness the flames
in the colours and contours
of an amazing secret.
All else is blank canvas,
the primal void, the vision in him
that turns toward the Sun.

(Phil Kelly b. Dublin 1950 d. Mexico City 2010)

LANDSCAPE WITH THE FALL OF ICARUS

An earlier dawn than usual
in the almostness of everything
which is late winter,
a year not yet itself.
Poets reach the narrow strand
between possibilities.
A scene is come upon:

The ploughman follows his furrow
as a shepherd looks at the sky.
Dog and sheep are content
to enact the pastoral scene,
not knowing they are Breughel's.
Here are the simple harmonies
faithfully framed.

As for Icarus,
failure is always happening,
as easily as the ship sails
into harbour with a cargo
of heroic verities,
including pain and solace.
Another dreamer is sure to rise.

DANCER

There is a silence that we may hear
in the music of motion's
exquisite geometries.

A spiral of fire as a phoenix rises.
A shower of ice when the tree shakes.

High towers cast shadows
where the wells were dry
in the city of white sky.

In the heat of the forest
the tigers are hunting,
but the bird in light air
is venturing sunward.

We are inside the machine,
believing what we see,
imagining everything
is happening now.

6. TIME PASSING

THERE IS NO TIME

We hear of time passing to the shore
of somewhere that is nowhere
beyond those signs more real
within lost dreams, our absence.
Still we may sleep when the clock stops.
There is no time to speak of
the future that has passed.
Leaves of wisdom drift down aimlessly.
The rotting timber reminds us
the price of prosperity
is measured in fire and flood.
There is no time to follow
the burning of the ice
and the incoming of oceans
when certain seasons fall.
Times change with the tides.

A GLANCE IN THE LOOKING GLASS

Stepping on the moving stair
an open mind seeks her heart
for fear of being mistaken.
Later a loner's lament echoes
on the subway walls.
He sings the same song again
that he may see his lost love.
She dare not meet his eyes.

There will be fruit to taste soon.
The juice as blood from battle flows
in the tidal swell of victory.
Once there was a silence in time,
a pause of origin unknown
going down an opening
so unexpectedly clear.

The shower of splinters glisten
in their many likelihoods
flowing through her mind.
There a child may fall

WAITING

The child waiting for the train,
her parents beside her,
has changed with the changing of trains,
and the ageing of her mother,
and the absence of her father
now waiting at another station.

What I saw then remains.
But the child is the haze
of fifteen summers later.
The songs she hears inside her.
She stands and sings
of many things that move her.

The music may be of memory,
perhaps of possibilities.
There are songs of waiting,
and then of being there,
especially when a child begins
to sing of anticipation.

The hope is universal:
a child is waiting for the train.

THE PROMISE

Dust blows in the dry winds,
darkening the lately fallen snow.
Brick and glass are scattered
as symbols of survival
when a plague of fire fell
in a cold winter war.
Torn flesh and raw bone are thrown
into the makeshift tombs,
One day there must be a memorial.
The living have vanished so soon.
Hope of return is left behind,
but life shall find its way again
when the enemy is silenced
by the peace that remains the promise.

CARTIER-BRESSON IN CAMERA

The transparent glass of past lives,
being no less than history
at the heart of things
where truth waits for acceptance.
The gods have an idea to share,
revealed reality turning to the sun
with a murmur of assent in the air.

All that is light can give
a sense of direction
to the mind's unease.
Various perceptions are seen
wandering the world.
Soon the stride stumbles
against an invisible wall.

We see no more
than endless reflections
moving beyond the bounds of reason.
Looking, we find ourselves
with uncertain expectations.
There is no conclusion
that time cannot fulfil.

CAMBRIDGE

Whereof one cannot speak
a clerkly sceptic may cast doubt
stumbling on the steps of conjecture.
In Pembroke Arch the voices echo
turning the stone to water.
The energy of intellect shimmers.
Many sights distract a casual eye
when light passes carelessly.
The gilt on a portal glistens
summoned to a thinker's conviction
burning through an original mind.
The sight is rare in any sky.

Birds settling on dry soil.
Thereof one must be silent
as ashes from everlasting fire,
where indifferent feet hasten,
the immortality scattered
before time will change the world.
The river runs its age-old course,
coiled in hope of eternity.
The truth is living here,
its several realities moving
in and out of hurried streets.
Rain falls here as everywhere.

SOUNDS UNSEEN

The door closes on the day.
From an open window
the air issues a warning,
but closure brings a sense of rest.
This house may feel at peace.

Outside there is an eager crowd
anticipating a journey.
They will not go far.
Inside there is no-one
beyond the eyes of her mind.

There is flesh on her face
beneath the silk that shields her
from the fire in the sky
and the ice that burns.
Nature is always there.

Some sounds remain unseen.
Others are visible in darkness.
Through the curtains a hint of light
that is the midnight watchword
never known to be silent.

THE AWAKENING OF STONE STATUES

'However great the movement of a sculpture may be....it must
return to itself, the great circle must complete itself, the circle of
solitude that encompasses a work of art.'
Rainer Maria Rilke *Auguste Rodin.*

A songbird's silent flight through the storm,
or the siren call to an unknown island,
the curfew cry in fading light,
with spell cast and runes read,
a task for Janus
gathering his spirit
fashioned by a curious fate,
familiar to the curious
who stand in the summer rain
and see the snow before it falls.

A trail of enchantment,
a picture chosen from many
for its muted tones.
Who determines the music's flow
through the fertile plains of the soul?
In every season there is something
to remember of another time.
When we feel spring's incoming
who dares not breathe in life?
The answers are carved in stone.

A FAMILY HISTORY

Because their memory is always
enveloping their presence
within the customary silence,
the sound that stirs is spectral.
History speaks of ancient names
in buried bones suddenly shaken
on uncertain ground.
I trace my fingers on inscriptions
faintly carved in stone
because there is always memory,
a gift from the earth,
When my spirit is stirred to remember,
defining the lie of the land
the spring in the hills flows down
with many kinds of water
among an ancestral eternity.
Theirs is the future because we live,
sweeping away the remaining dust
to reveal their memory as always.

WHAT MEANING MEANS

In the public gardens
there are faces by the fountains,
still, solemn, solitary,
They sit as memorials
to the closing of doors,
the darkening of windows.

There are things that befell her shadow
in the suddenness of day
that she dare not ask why.
The grass grew wild
in the old street stones.
Shards of window pane
shatter underfoot.
She was thinking of a poor child
in her hopscotch of memory.

The trees in the garden
may dance with her plans
when her dream arranges travelling
for her soul to sing in basilicas
and her eye to linger on frescos
and her hand to touch the grandeur
of all the ancient places.
And her feet to discover
the other side of cities.

And so to push at an opening door
toward the elders' temptation

of kindly faces beckoning
all the poor children
along lost corridors
where innocence collides.
In her private garden
we find infinite space.

WHEN WILL THEY RETURN?

How the trees have fallen.
When will they return?
A question answered
by the cutting blade
of the house that was
long since abandoned
to improve the prospect
when a new house rose
in place of what was
another, known well.

So clearly regretted,
though I have imagined
how it might be again,
an impossible comeback
a return that is no more
that for ever is never,
even when saplings grow.
A death before dying
as the roots must wither,
when they went elsewhere,
like skeletons of memory,
there to remain many years,
and where shall the sparrows nest
if a sense of loss lingers....
as another spring approaches?
I speak of growing hope.
When young we may believe
that this is an eternity

in nature's promise
of always being how things are
in the picture of reality
then they change without asking.
The colours we see soon fade.
Living becomes so unexpected,
I stand in silence,
subject to sudden movements
wondering where to go
when the earth shakes and cracks
as if the end of all has come
and we know no more….
of what we knew of here.

THE TIME OF MY LIFE

In the early morning at first light it may seem that the stones come
alive. They may appear to move or to speak. Of course it is only
the mist of a grey dawn. Or perhaps there was a spirit within the
uncarved stone, a spirit waiting for release. And so the statues wait
for the moment they can sigh if not sing, and quiver if not dance.
A distant clock strikes the hour. The resonance speaks, so it seems,
not of time passing but of eternity. Flesh soon withers, whereas
stone sees many ages pass by in the rise and fall of empires and
epochs.

Dying, I lose all sense of time,
being one with the universe
until my eyes open in suffering.
The pain recedes, leaving me young again,
but not as young as I become
when as a child I play,
finding innocence by degrees
on my journey to the womb.
Before that there is love
gaining on me all the time.

A GUIDE FOR TRAVELLERS

There is a land of conjecture
where truth ripens for all believers.
Its roots go down to the core
that is the source of meaning.
I write with good intentions
and a sense of direction
only to be found in a state of loss
where fellow travellers have gone.
My pen may make the crossing
over the rumoured realms
always with the morning star.
The mountains appear to move
and vanish in a haze
even on those clearer days.
Some are certain they know the way,
yet cannot agree the terrain
with its tracks leading nowhere
or returning in a circle
that the hours of dark define
as a tasting of temptations
in lightest harmony
when travellers sigh,
a symptom of arrival
housed among shadows,
But the east is scarlet.
And sky is never pure blue

MORE THAN POSSIBLE

Among the uncertainties
waiting to be abandoned
with no earthly ambition
when an open door reveals
what was never there
at midnight in innocence
so to see the sun rise
for want of clear light
where may be found lost souls
who had walked this way
among the remains
in the colour of silence
where layers of feeling retain
the endless questioning
from behind another depth,
the surface slowly defining
nothing more than possible.

PENNILESS PORCH

The mayfly hovers in Needle's Eye
when a bell sounds the time
as long as the plough turns bones,
restless in the fecund ground.
The cathedral choir is seen
floating in the hills.
History falls where it will.
Consider the saintly ones.
Under the cedars they find
leaves scattered in the rain.
A breaking branch reveals
their trials not yet ending.

So many prayers have passed
in the irreverent air.
Pastures are green again
when frost is burned in the sun.
A fox trail in the levels drove,
fresh imprints disappearing.
Lichen on the churchyard tombs.
In a lifetime are many lives.
Here lie the carnival queens
forever attended by elemental earth.
And further out the horses run
the long finger stretching westerly.

OF ALL WORDS

Love is the least known
of everything spoken,
of all words the strangest
among the familiar.
We think we know what we mean,
though life is more
than the rhythm of the heart
when there are essentials voiced
with feeling in the dark well down.
We may hear no more of her
but an echo of her truth
that is beyond our reach.

And the thought of her becomes
another time entirely
where falls no rain but gently
on the parasol shade opened
for the sun rising.

There the water glistens
in supplicant eyes seeing.
The sound inside has no words but hers.
For the word that is hers is true,
a promise waiting to be heard.